shades

of

sorrow

sabina laura

Copyright © Sabina Laura
All rights reserved.

No portion of this book may be used or reproduced without written permission from the author except for the use of brief quotation in book reviews or scholarly journals.

Edited by Shelby Leigh

ISBN: 9798838170286

this is how it feels

when the light fades

(and comes back again).

this is a breaking apart

(and a falling back together).

this is a reach into the space

between hurting and healing

(and finding that *so much exists there).*

dusk

- 1 -

midnight

- 47 -

dawn

- 93 -

dusk

when the horizon

darkened until

no light remained,

i lost myself

to the night

and all her different

shades of sorrow.

i spend too long
visiting this museum
of all the things
that didn't stay,
keeping the souvenirs
like unlucky charms
and leaving fingerprints
on the glass.

i'm tired of gaining memories
that always come from
losing something.

i am an unfinished poem.

a folded corner of a page
waiting to be found again.

a sunrise hidden
by thick fog.

lungs trying to claw
their way out.
(it is easier than breathing).

and i am all broken bones
and grazed skin,
left to collect dust as if

it
doesn't
even
matter.

you'd think
i'd be used to it by now,
the way some days take so much
and give so little.

but still,
morning arrives too violently,
leaves bruises beneath heavy eyelids.

and when i say
it's because i didn't get much sleep,
what i really mean is
i wish the days were a little kinder.

don't be fooled
by appearances —

my smile has held
both everything
and nothing
within it,
and always looked
the same
from the outside.

i fear
i am wilting
before i ever truly bloomed,
but that's the trouble with time:

there's never quite as much as you think.

we try
to ignore
the ache.

shove it
at the bottom
of the dirty laundry pile.

shut it
between the pages
of our favourite book.

sweep it
under the carpet
and pretend it isn't there.

leave it
at home, and instead,
grab our smile on the way out.

did life think
it was a kindness

to show me the open sky
through the bars of this cage?

to me,
it feels nothing but cruel.

but then,
how can you possibly decide

whether it is better
to see something beautiful

and know it will always be
out of reach

or to never even know
it existed at all?

i count the seconds
in raindrops against the windowsill,
an echo of sky clouding over my eyes,
but how slow every day feels
while waiting for the sun.

i taught myself
to keep everyone
at arm's length
so they couldn't
break my heart,

but i was unaware
of how easily
safe distances
can rearrange
into loneliness.

it all seems to darken
under the shadow of a question mark,

hovering above everything like a bird
that cannot remember how to fly,
but refuses to land
in case it looks like failure.

if i rewind twenty years,
i am still full of questions.

they are simpler ones, i admit —
eased by the comfort of the nest,
the shelter of the trees.

but all the same —
wanting, waiting, wondering.

and if i fast forward to now,
i am still so empty of answers.

this eagerness
to grasp each day
has left me trying
to fit the whole sky
in my palms
and crushing
what little light
there is.

I HAVE FOUND

THAT PAIN

HAS A HABIT

OF PLANTING

ROOTS

IN BEAUTIFUL

HEARTS.

i still carry suitcases full of memories
about people who do not think of me
and i write them postcards that i do not send.

i hold my hands out for people
who do not even look in my direction
and i always give more than i get.

because i do not settle for halfway;
instead, i go miles just to knock on doors
that do not open.

you are every sunrise
i couldn't wait to meet
and every sunset
i didn't want to leave

and somehow you feel
like a beginning
and an ending
rolled into one.

in a dream
i am seventeen again.

the soft heart i wear on my sleeve
is a little naïve at the edges,

but nothing too bad
has made a home in me yet.

in a dream
i am seventeen again.

it is the last sweet year,
but i am blissfully unaware.

i cannot imagine a tomorrow
that isn't bursting with light.

my bones are breaking
under the weight
of my own expectations.

i pile too much on
and then wonder why
i cannot move.

there are no oceans between us,
no countries,
not even that many miles.

but there is time,
and somehow,
that is the greatest distance of all.

anyone who has ever felt
any kind of pain
doesn't want to hear you say
everything happens for a reason.

- sometimes positivity is toxic

we notice in autumn
that something is missing.

uncertainty blankets the future
like an early morning fog.

the emptiness of the trees
becomes an uncomfortable mirror.

and i am afraid
we will not survive the winter.

i only know
how to measure time now
by the changing skyline,
watching each day fade
to black.

yet still,
i am grateful
for this shift.

because time is
the only part of my world
that hasn't stopped moving.

i did not realise
how easily
hands could let go.

i did not realise
how much
it would hurt when they did.

- *until you*

i am a shivering baby bird in the nest
with april shower-soaked wings.

there is no song in my throat,
just another apology.

the things i love
are always leaving,
like a setting sun
into a hungry horizon.

they tell me that every day
brings a newness,
so i search at each dawn,
but sometimes, all i find is mourning.

so although the sun still rises,
it seems as though
everything that gives us light
also casts a shadow.

loneliness has a way
of tricking you into thinking
you need to fill all the empty spaces
with people who don't belong.

- why i let you back in

i retrace the same thoughts
a thousand times,
spinning around in circles
until i become dizzy.

it seems that the only direction
i know how to move
is falling back into habits
i thought i had grown out of.

i build fear
like a mountain
and turn every river
into an ocean,
and when the rain
begins to fall,
i cannot help but think
that the sun will never return.

love should not feel
like an open wound.
a closed door.
an in-between.

love should not leave you
reaching and reaching
and reaching.

I SPENT MY LIFE

LEARNING TO FLY

FOR MY WINGS

TO BREAK

AS SOON AS

I WAS READY.

like mistaking salt
for sugar,

you looked a lot like love,
but you weren't.

i am the empty river
that cannot remember
the touch of rain,

that dried up in summer
while the rest of the world
danced under waterfalls.

i am the bare tree waiting for springtime,
surrounded by the pink cherry blossom
of those who found a way to grow.

i am the wolf that howls at the moon
and the hawk that circles for hours,
just searching for a way to survive.

because i know the word for *longing*
in every language.
it is the only breath left in my lungs.

this heart is
all or nothing.

if you ask me
to loosen my grip,
i will let you go
entirely.

i did not see it coming:

the sudden silence
without even a fading echo.
the cutting of all ties
without even a warning
that they were strained.

because you left in a way
that made closure
almost impossible,
that meant the only chance
i had of healing would be
to do the same:

to bury you in the past
so your ghosting
could not haunt me
anymore.

i think about letting go,

but how do i break us apart
without feeling the shatter?

how do i leave us behind
without feeling the loss?

i have not worn an age
this heavy before,
but grief has aged me
far more than time.

- *twenty-seven*

we said we would never
let the distance
shape into silence.

we said we would never
let the silence
shape into goodbye.

- broken promises

how many times will i go back
to what has hurt me
because i am scared to be alone?

when will i learn
that the bridges only leading to pain
are better off being burnt?

SABINA LAURA

HOW CAN

LONELINESS

STILL

FIND ME

IN A ROOM

FULL OF

GHOSTS?

dusk yawns
and the day slowly falls away,
but time has always had a way
of leaving before i can hold it,
of making centuries disappear
between each lost second.
and although i am not ready
to let go of another day,
deep down i know
it was never mine to keep.
all i can do is watch helplessly
as the shadows on the wall grow longer,
and all i can think is how they look like
a dream coming to an end.

autumn exhales
and the trees lose
another piece
of themselves.

i know that
something beautiful
will eventually replace
what has been lost,

but in this moment,
all i feel is the emptiness
and how it seems to stretch out
endlessly.

i wonder, what have i gained
from all this holding back?
instead of just jumping into the sea
without a second thought, i wait —
listen to anxiety whisper in my ear,
tell me that the water is too cold,
that i could drown,
that there could be sharks.
and so, (as always),
hesitation becomes refusal.
i cling to the safety of the sand
and watch the others enjoy
what the ocean has to give.
but then, a far more important question
rolls in with the waves,
and i wonder, what have i *lost*
from all this holding back?
it seems that all along,
the sharks were only in my mind.

they say
there is hope
on the horizon,
but that is too far
out of reach
and the sun
is rapidly setting.

midnight

there are moments
that shouldn't feel sad,
like knowing sunrise
will come back for me.

but all i can think is:
the ache will still be here tomorrow.

i wait
but grief still sits
in the corner
of every room.

i wait
but grief has lungs,
a heartbeat,
grows into an everlasting thing.

i wait
but eventually,
time becomes
another wound.

i have been trying
to twist outcomes into shapes
i hope will be more gentle,
but now everything has become
moulded by these rituals.
because i have convinced myself
that fate is in my hands,
that my world will fall apart
if i stop holding it together.
and although deep down
i know i cannot write
my own future,
i am terrified
of what may be lost
if i let go.

I KNOW

THE SADNESS

COMES IN WAVES

BUT I DON'T KNOW

HOW TO BREATHE

UNDERWATER

ON THE DAYS

IT FEELS LIKE

A TSUNAMI.

tucked quietly away
in the attic of my mind
are the hidden things —

the things we don't talk about,
the things we try to forget,
the things we cannot look in the eye,

and although sometimes i cannot help
but think about saying goodbye
to the ghosts that live here,

there's a part of me
that wants
to be haunted.

when i look at my fears
through a magnifying glass,
i am forced to acknowledge
that sometimes,
i am the architect
of my own suffering.
that sometimes, the war
is only in my mind.
because i convince myself
that everything is unfolding
in the worst way,
and i let the chaos consume me
long before logic can catch up.

all my dreams
are buried
under an avalanche
and all my nightmares
seep into dawn
and stain the day,
but i have been
sleepwalking
for so long now
that i'm afraid
there's no hope
of ever waking up.

depression is an oil spill
in a once vibrant ocean.

it unfolds throughout every part
and leaves nothing untouched.

inside,
i twist
into shapes.

my chest
ties up
in knots.

agony
tangles itself
between the ribs.

all the air
leaves
my lungs.

and i wonder,
is this still a heartbeat?
or just a throbbing pain?

i have carried this sorrow with me
for so long, i think i would feel lost
without it. because it's a part of me now,
just like the bones that hold me together
and the lungs that help me breathe.

this is not to say there hasn't been joy;
there has been so much. but through it all,
the depression does not let go.
even the happiest moments
have still carried some shards of sadness.

what if,
when joy looks briefly
in my direction,
i do not even recognise her?

what if
the light at the end of the tunnel
is just an illusion,
just hope playing tricks on me?

because what if
it doesn't get better?
what if this is nothing
but a slow death?

everything comes with
an expiration date

which is to say

everything decays almost
as soon as it has finished ripening

which is to say

everything leaves before
i have finished loving it.

i see the world
through different eyes now,
ones that only know
of black and white,
but the hardest part
is that everyone keeps telling me
the world is so full of colour.

anxiety
sinks its teeth in.

eats away
at the softest flesh
and spits it
back out.

kisses the wound
better, then says
it was only ever
in my head.

depression is
a paperweight
against my lungs.

an unnecessary gravity
pulling down my bones.

an unwanted anchor
tied to my chest.

and the weight
of every day
feels the same;

always too much.

my eyes are wide open

but all i see is darkness,

and my hands keep searching

but all i find are empty spaces.

the future looks like
a winter sky,
all colourless and clouded and
s   t   r   e   t   c   h   i   n   g
out into nothing.

the butterflies
that have made
a permanent home in my chest
are not the gentle kind.
their wings have sharp edges
that dig in every time
i try to inhale
and they do not flutter.
instead, they dash and dart
and leave me restless.

i am homesick
for normality,

but how easy it is
to take something
for granted
when you do not realise
it can leave.

grief is the skeleton of me.

what i mean is that
nothing holds my bones
quite like loss.

everything seems
to hurt more than
it should.

it's like one small
unexpected snowflake
suddenly becomes an avalanche.

it's like there is no such thing
as a papercut anymore —
i am always covered in blood.

it's like i have forgotten
the colour grey and i can only see
black and white.

it's like everything either
kisses the wound better
or rips it right open.

i swore
i wouldn't write
any more poems
about you,

but every word
just seems to become
another way of saying
i miss you.

i am holding another funeral
for something else i used to be,

because it seems as though
every garden i ever grew
has turned into a graveyard
and every gravestone is engraved
with the name of something else i've lost.

it seems as though
my hands have become cemeteries
for all the things i could not hold on to
and mirrors only show
everything i wanted to be.

it seems as though
every moment is another step closer
to the end of something else,
and i am afraid there aren't
any new beginnings left.

when the anxiety sets in,
i become a kaleidoscope
of fractured breaths, spiralling
into colours i only see
when the world is ending.

even with eyes closed
i am restless.

even under a midnight sky
i cannot tell the difference
between daydreams and nightmares,

and all these sleepless nights
leave me aching
for a stillness
that never comes.

THERE IS

AN OCEAN

OF SORROW

STRETCHING OUT

IN FRONT OF ME

AND IT IS HARD

NOT TO THINK

ABOUT DROWNING.

i have to relearn
the word *forgiveness*
a thousand times a day,
try to give it the space it deserves
by forcing anger to become smaller.
and i know that life does not
promise anybody softness,
but i am far too fragile
for this many sharp edges.

tears land on my pillow
like a rainstorm in the night
and the sun has not
shown herself in days.
they tell me *it gets better*
if you just give it time,
but i know that morning
will only bring more rain.

i didn't know
how to love you
without overflowing
and you didn't know
how to love me
at all.

when they think
of depression
as a winter day,
it is fresh and white
instead of grey,
sparkling snow
instead of endless fog,
as if the sun
will come back,
as if spring is only
around the corner,
as if everything here
hasn't already died
long ago.

i have been searching
for somewhere to land
but it seems that the sadness
knows how to hold me
better than anything else.

i carried shame with me for so long,
held it like an umbrella,
hoped it would keep the storms away.
and when it didn't, shame convinced me
that i was a failure. so i learnt
to wear sunshine on the outside
even though i couldn't remember
how to feel anything but rain.
but that still wasn't enough.
shame demanded to know
where the sadness grew from,
as if i was watering it intentionally,
as if i could just find the root and dig it out.
but i had a whole garden
buried within my chest,
and so shame begged me
to keep it a secret.

the fog doesn't lift.

the frost doesn't clear.

depression's gift.

winter
all
year.

loneliness used to be
an empty room,
but it was an empty room
within a home.
now, everything has left
and i am an abandoned city.
all that remains
are the crumbling ruins
of memory.

this heart
looks like autumn.

the wind howls
with longing
and the leaves fall
from the trees
like tears.

the future
is full of fear.

the past
is full of grief.

and everything in between
is slipping through my fingers
before i can hold on to it.

i planted seeds in my mind
and watered them daily,
but now i cannot stop them
from growing.

- *the root of anxiety*

i am afraid
that this wanting
does not know
where to end,
that this mouth
has forgotten
the taste of *thank you,*
that if you place
a sliver of moonlight
in my palms
i will crush
the entire sky.

ANXIETY

GIVES ME

TOO MUCH

SPACE

TO THINK

AND

NEVER ENOUGH

SPACE

TO BREATHE.

i wonder,
how many silent ways
can i break
before someone looks
in my direction?

my dreams
look like
a collection
of all the moments
that are now
missing from me,

and i fear
they're all i have left.

when i say
everything looks like an ending,

i mean
that the future looks bruise-coloured
like a sky ready to say goodnight.

i mean
that any moment could be a last time
and we wouldn't know until it was too late.

i mean
that even if you're not looking for a way out
life can still keep showing you exit signs.

the sun rises
again
like a habit
we do not know
how to break,
but it makes
no difference.

from here
the world is dimly lit,
no matter the hour,
no matter the season.

dawn

i think
i will always be
half a breath
between
the hurting
and the healing.

i can't wait
to see what happens
when i plant enough courage
to tell the stories
i have kept hidden,
when i open my heart
like a budding flower,
and when i learn to accept
the rain-soaked parts of me,

because i know this blooming
will be beautiful.

i no longer

fear the dark.

the night is home

to so many

beautiful things

and i have

a nocturnal heart.

i will not let heartbreak
make me a stranger to love
and i will not let loneliness
make me reach out to toxic people.
i will not let fear steal
every moment of peace
and i will not let sadness steal
every flicker of joy.
i will keep searching
for the good in everything,
and i will find it.
i will find it.

i had become so used
to the rain you poured over me,
that when you left
i couldn't help
but miss the storm.

but in time i realised
not everyone you lose is a loss —
sometimes it just takes
a little time to notice
that the sun has come back.

the days and nights
merge into one
until they blur,
but there is
a much needed
softness to life
when it is out of focus.
after all, the details
are not always kind.

there's no need to feel bad
if you spent all day on the sofa,
kept the curtains drawn,
cancelled meeting your friends,
forgot to shower,
cried yourself to sleep.

today is made of only survival,
and that's okay.

there will be days ahead
when living is possible again.

i am not fading
like i feared.

i refuse to.

i am more vibrant
than ever.

there will always be rain,
but here's the thing:

you cannot let it drown you.
you cannot let it convince you
that the sun will not return.

you have to find a way through.
dance in it, if you feel brave enough.
sing loudly of gratitude until
you no longer hear the thunder.
take shelter when you need to.
build an umbrella out of joy.
plant seeds of hope while the earth is soft.

because there will always be rain,
but let it fall. let it stay.
let it be the reason you flourish.

i hope one day
i cannot remember
how the walls
of this cage feel.

i hope one day
i have enough space
to unfold myself
in all the ways i'd like.

my heart lives
on the wrong side of today,
but i'm just searching
for all the dreams i've lost.

and when they tell me
to look to the future,
i know i'd rather keep
my head in the clouds.

the view from here
is beautiful.

i am still learning
how to love a body
that lets me down like this.

i am still learning
how to settle in a body
that does not feel like a home.

- acceptance is a work in progress

these days,
the ache
is quieter.
i still hear it,
but it is mostly
background noise,
and i am getting good
at turning up the volume
of everything else.

these days,
the ache
takes up less room
than it used to.
it is still there,
hiding in the shadows
of every room,
but i am getting good
at looking the other way.

i have worn my heart
on my sleeve for too long,
let it dirty at the hem,
let the stitches unravel.

i always hope
others will be gentle with it,
but first, i must learn
to do the same.

kindness is such a necessary thing,
because i fear that everyone is
fighting battles they don't talk about.
i fear that everyone is
carrying far more weight
than their delicate shoulders
were made for.

i have grown tired
of seeking light.

storms bring change
and i love the way
the sky feels
before it rains.

SABINA LAURA

SOME

PAIN

STAYS,

BUT

WE

LEARN

TO

CARRY

IT.

my bones
haven't yet fractured
under the weight
of a bad day,
like an oak tree
standing strong
throughout the storms.

and even though
i have lost my leaves,
i still have
the roots,
the branches,
the soil,
the open sky above me.

because there is still so much to be found here.
there are still so many ways i can grow.

pain and joy are always competing to be felt,
and while they take it in turns,
neither are ever absent.

so although this heart may break
in a thousand different ways,
it heals in a million more.

to self-doubt,

you chipped away at me for years,
moulding me into a smaller version of myself.
then you laughed. you'd been right all along:
i would never amount to anything.

you questioned whatever i said and did,
making me wish i could become invisible.
then you smirked. you'd been right all along:
i would never be noticed by anyone.

but i am not listening to you anymore,
because i am finally realising
that you do not speak the truth,
and you no longer get to hold me back.

don't be afraid
to show the parts of you
that hurt the most,

because vulnerability
doesn't look like weakness;
it looks like *w a r r i o r*.

my head lives in the clouds,
and my heart does, too,
and when i watch the way
they always change shape,
i know there is still hope.
because i am getting good
at reshaping my dreams,
at finding abstract
in the absence of concrete.
i am still finding ways
to discover fullness
even though so much is missing.

despite pain.

despite grief.

despite sorrow.

there can still be joy.

i am tired of anxiety
weaving its way
through every chapter.

i am tired of knowing
it will be there tomorrow
before i even turn the page.

so now, i am trying to write
the rest of my story without fear
as the main character.

only i am in control of the ink.

there is
no shame
in sadness.

even the moon
isn't always full
and has to go through phases.

even the earth
falls dark
and has to wait for dawn.

even the trees
lose their leaves
and have to grow again.

there is something beautiful
about the way hearts heal.
it is slow, yes,
and it is messy, too,
but time is the most gentle stitching
for even the deepest of wounds.

when the night
is a hurting thing,
i remember:

there are new days coming,
petal soft and honey sweet.

note to self:

not everything will leave.

even a sunrise
can look like a sunset
to eyes that only know
of endings.

i have come to love
the weeds and thorns
that plant roots
within me.

they are proof that
i am still a growing thing.

the night will break
open eventually,
revealing all the light
you could possibly need.
new dreams will replace
the broken ones.
happiness will no longer
feel like a distant memory.
and you will be reminded
of all the reasons why
you kept holding on.

somewhere through
all the sadness and confusion,
i realised that i needed to accept
you weren't coming back,

and somewhere through
all the self-doubt and questions,
i realised that *the way you left
does not define my worth.*

dear self,

for the times
i didn't show you enough love,

for the times
i didn't love you at all,

i forgive you.

i have lost myself
too many times to count
and i'm not sure
i ever truly know
where i'm going,
but i'm learning
that this journey
is less about
where we end up
and more about
all the hands we hold
along the way.

i do not want violence
to be a language
i speak to myself in.

let this be a softening.
let this be a white flag.

dear depression,

you can try

to empty the sky

of all its light

but i will still be here,

counting every star

that shines through the dark.

i found my way
through the fog
and finally saw
how beautiful life can be
out in the open.

this is not to say
there will never be
another misty morning,
but this time
i know it will
eventually clear.

courage has always felt too heavy
to hold in my hands.
fear has been easier —
so easy that i have never needed
to reach for it at all.

but i have been brave.

i have fought battles in secret
and still won, even without an army.
i have been weighed down by grief
and still put one foot in front of the other.
i have rebuilt joy from scratch
and created kingdoms.

but that's the thing:
i have not lived without fear,
and i never will.

i have lived despite it.

there will be days full
of fireplace warmth and sunshine laughter,
smiles that have nothing to hide
and hands that have plenty to hold.

there will be days when
you forget to remember the ache,
where agony leaves the room
and shuts the door behind her.

and there will be days when
you see sunrise as a celebration
and when you wake to the sound
of the birds singing, you'll want to join in.

and i promise you,
they'll be worth the wait.

there is
an undeniable
emptiness,
but maybe
i was wrong
for trying
to fill it.
maybe it's okay
to leave
a little room
to breathe.

sometimes,
change is as slow as
one season falling
into the next
and as gentle as
the earth spinning
on its axis.
so although
it may seem like
nothing is moving,
in time, everything
will feel a little warmer
and look a little brighter,
and you will realise
that all along,
you were healing.

thank you for giving my words a home

follow on social media: @sabinalaurapoetry

Also by Sabina:

Moonflower

All This Wild Hope

Silver Linings:
poetry, affirmations, & gentle reminders

A little sunshine and a little rain:
A Poetry Journal

Printed in Great Britain
by Amazon